I0170433

FRUITS FROM MY HEART

Carolyn Walker Odell

Tandem Light Press

Tandem Light Press
950 Herrington Rd.
Suite C128
Lawrenceville, GA 30044

Tandem Light Press paperback edition July 2015

ISBN: 978-0-9861660-8
Library of Congress Control Number: 2015936327

PRINTED IN THE UNITED STATES OF AMERICA

*This book is dedicated in loving memory of
my parents, William and Bessie Walker, and
to the important people in my life-
my husband, my daughter, my family/friends, and
my Christian family*

CONTENTS

Section I: Spiritual

Section II: Love

Section III: Other Inspirations

INTRODUCTION

I have been writing for years and wanted to leave a legacy for my family, friends, and to those who have an interest in poetry. I love to share my creativity and hope to bring joy and inspiration to others. I also hope that through poetry, I can facilitate the Christian faith of God and love in others.

Sometimes life can seem to bring great challenges but none are superior to God and his love for us along with our love for each other. I believe that at the end of life, we will all discover that it was about love and God is love.

SECTION I

SPIRITUAL

GOD'S MISSION FOR CHRISTIANS

Did you ever wonder what your mission in life is?
What does God want you to do?
Accept Jesus Christ as your risen Savior.
Believe in the Lord with all your heart, mind, and soul.
Admit you are a sinner, and ask God to forgive you for your sins.
Be baptized for the death of your sins.
Study your Bible daily; go to Bible study and Sunday School.
Attend church services regularly.
Learn all you can about the Lord.
Put on your Christian armor.
Be quick to forgive.
Love others like you love yourself.
Visit the sick, visit the imprisoned, and feed the poor.
Praise God, and compliment people.
Reach out with kindness and love to others.
God is love. If you love others, God is in you.
Try hard to keep peace and be at peace with yourself.
Lean on the Lord. Trust him.
Tell him all of your problems and joys.
Pray daily and God will reveal all to you.
He will lead you and guide you and you will know your mission.
Have faith. It is powerful.

Love and faith together will stamp out your fears for fear is often not a good emotion.
Keep God as the centerpiece in your life; put Him first.
Smile, be happy, joyful, and pass it on to others.

GOD'S AWESOME CREATION

I looked up at the clear blue sky.
I watched the birds spread their
wings and glide, gathering in flocks and gradually disappearing.
I heard their tweeting song slowly dissipate.
Oh, how wonderful is God's creation, I thought.
Then I peered out over the turquoise ocean, surrounded
by bleached white sand.
I heard the sounds of the vast waters like a roaring lion.
The waves bounced with intensity into a foamy splash.
The water covered my bare feet.
I could feel the coldness and crumbly bits of sand.
I gazed at an eternity of water and sky that stole my
mind into meditation for a while.
This is God's magnificent creation, I thought.
In a deep breath, I inhaled its beauty.
Again, I pondered for a moment and wondered how
God came up with such a beautiful painting by his fingertips.
I whispered, "He's awesome."

THERE'S A WAR GOING ON

Hush, hush, you better stop, look and listen, watch and pray.
The devil's on the loose and trying to lead you astray.
Put on your Godly armor so you can stand firm
and not land with the evil spirits of the unseen dark world.
Put on your spiritual boxing gloves.
You'll need to fight against evil rulers, the powers of darkness of
this world.
Remain faithful to God and the battle will certainly be won.
He will provide you with all you need to put the devil and evil
behind you.

Hush, hush, you better stop, look and listen, watch, and pray.
There's a spiritual war going on, there's a war going on.
Keep your faith in our Lord God
and you'll certainly win the battle.
He's the One on High; there's no greater One than Jesus Christ,
Our Lord.

GOING HOME, HOME, HOME, HOME

I've lived my time out.
Now I'm next in line,
The Lord's calling my name.
I can't live here the same.
I've packed my bag, got my coat on my arm.
Good-bye, good-bye, good-bye
I'm going home, home, home, home
I'm going home.

I see the bright streets of gold.
Just like the stories I've been told.
Crystal clear rain coming down and up through the fountains.
You know there'll be no more pain or darkness over there.
Beautiful green trees lined by the crystal clear river.
The Lord's calling my name.
I can't live here the same.
Good-bye, good-bye, good-bye
I'm going home, home, home, home
I'm going home.

LORD, I NEED A HEALING

Lord, I need a healing today.
What do you say?
For my mind, my body, and my spirit!
Lord, I need a healing!
Oh Lord, I need a healing!

Lord, I'm hurting, filled with
anger, no forgiveness, and bitterness!

Lord, my mother, my father, my
children, and friends too, have all let me down.

Lord, my body is weakened
and swelling with pain!

Lord, I trust in you to heal my mind, body, and spirit
for with faith in you, all things are possible and
I don't have to worry about a thing.

Please remember:
Oh Lord, I need a healing!

LORD, PLEASE GIVE ME LOVE

Lord, please give me love.
Fill me up, let it overflow, overflow, in your name.
Love, love, love, way down deep, that's what I want.

Lord, please don't let me sound like loud brass
or a squeaky cymbal, making a lot of noise and all that stuff.
Lord, please give me more than high knowledge
and faith that can move mountains.

Lord, please let me do more than give to the poor,
sharing my material things.

Lord, please let me be patient, kind, gentle—
slow to anger and fear no evil.

For without love, Lord,
everything else, is in vain, in vain, in vain.
I want to be like you, Jesus.
Please hear my humble plea.
Love, love, love, that's what I want.
Love for everybody, that's what I want.

I WILL TRUST IN THE WILL OF GOD

God lifted me out of the dark pit of sin.
He set my feet on His solid ground.
He picked me up and out of the
mud and sinking mire.

I will trust in the will of God.

He has shown me the right path to take,
In the light where He empowers me.

I will trust in the will of God.

See how God has molded me.
He does just what I've been told.
Put your trust in Him,
and you will truly be amazed
at what He will do for you.
When I feel sad and discouraged,

I put my trust in the will of God.

I give him the praise because
He's my Savior, my Lord God.

I will trust in the will of God.

THE LORD LOVES US

He loves me, He loves you
and his love is everlasting.

He loves me, He loves you
and his love is unfailing.

He loves me, He loves you
and his love is inseparable.

He loves me, He loves you
His love is kind, gentle, and comforting.

He loves me, He loves you
His love is pure, sure, and true.

He loves me, He loves you
His love is firm, and immoveable.

He loves me, He loves you.
I'm so glad the Lord truly loves us and we belong to Him.
The Lord loves us.
Yes, He loves us.
He loves us.

YOU NEED TO TRUST IN GOD

When you are not sure, just what to do,
You need to trust in God.

When you're faced with burdens, tests, and tribulations,
You need to trust in God.

When you are lonely, sad, and fear that no one really cares,
You need to trust in God.

When you are jealous and envious of others and always
comparing yourself,
You need to trust in God.

When you are sick, I mean really sick, and think you
might be in your last days,
You need to trust in God.

When you are tired, and feel like it's all too much
and you are just about ready to give up,
You need to trust in God.

Trust in God!
When you're are not sure just what to do,
Trust in God!

TELL ME TO GO

Jesus, oh Jesus,
tell me to go, go, go, go
down on my knees
to repent of my sins.

Jesus, oh Jesus,
tell me to believe in You
with all my heart, mind, and soul.

Jesus, oh Jesus,
tell me to watch and pray, and
be ready when You return.

Jesus, oh Jesus
tell me that you love me
and you know all about me.

Jesus, oh Jesus
tell me I can call on You
in my time of need, any hour, any day.

Jesus, oh Jesus
tell me to go, go, go, go
down on my knees.

WHEN YOU FEEL LIKE

When you feel like you can't go any further,
remember that God says He will not put too much on us.

Think about a time when things were going really well, this will happen again. When you feel like no one cares about what's bothering you, get down on your knees and pray. God will not turn His ears away.

Go to that person that you want to hear your story, ask them for a time to chat; they too may have heavy burdens to bare.
When you start to feel sorry for yourself, know that you will not be a victim.

Think about a challenging time that God brought you through.
The strong survive the best, and you have strengths unknown.

When your energy gets low, don't lie down – go for a walk, or ride a bicycle.
All that extra junk needs to get out of your blood stream and you will feel more relaxed as the good enzymes flow.

Take a vacation if you can; get away from stressful
and trifling things.
Enjoy life, and when you return, the pictures of life
will not be blurry.

Some way, the needed fuel returns that allows you to pick up and continue the paths, crooks, and turns, ice cream, and strawberries, that are part of life's journey.

Seek His face through faith and you will see open doors,
beautiful gateways that the sun shines brightly through
Murky clouds leaking a vestige of hope. Use your talents and gifts; they are always needed.

PRAISE JESUS 'TIL THE END

I'm going to praise Jesus 'til the end of my time
With my mouth
I'm going to praise Him with my Mouth.

With my heart
I'm going to praise Him with all of my heart.

With my mind
I'm going Praise Him with all of my mind.

With all of my Soul
I'm going to praise Him with all my soul
From deep down within my soul.

With love and obedience
I'm going to praise Him with love and obedience.

With song and praise
I'm going to praise Him with song and praise.
He is most worthy to be praised.

CHRISTIANS, DON'T MAKE EXCUSES

Come on, Christians, don't make excuses!
You know you've got to live right!

You can't continue to live in sin!
Don't keep doing wrong.
When you know how to do right!

Jesus knows a tree by the fruit it bears.
Don't let anyone fool you.
Jesus knows your heart, mind, and soul.

Confess your sins; throw them all away!
Love one another.
Show your love to the Lord
by obeying his commandments.
Pray every day.
Ask the Holy Spirit to empower you.
Sing praises in our Lord's name
and you'll never be the same!

A CRY UP IN HEAVEN

Let me tell you a story about a young man.
He was a married man.
His wife came to him one day and said,
"We're going to have a child.
I'm going to call him, Michael; just what I call you."
The young man smiled and said, "I'm going be a daddy.
That little boy is going to be just like me."
When the baby came, it was a boy and they called his name,
Michael.
The young man looked at the little baby and smiled.
He looked up toward the heavens and said,
"Thank you, Jesus, for this precious God sent child."

When the child was one year old, the young man heard
A cry up in heaven. He said it like this:
The angels are at the pearly gates calling for little Michael.
Too young to know sin, too young to know life, but not too young
for God almighty to place him under the angel's wings, angel's
wings.
God's taking His child back.
He loves him the best.

The angels are singing, and kneeling and taking him up under their wings. One day, one day, we'll see each other again at the pearly gates.

I heard a cry up in Heaven.

I WONDER WHAT HE WOULD SAY

When I shake Sister Pat's hand, I smile real big, but I didn't really want to. I don't even like her.
Under my smile lies a real frown.
I wonder what He would say if He knew what I was thinking.

And look over there at Sister Henrietta and that good looking man on her arm. How did she get him? I'm prettier than she. Why, just yesterday I told them what a nice couple they make, but I didn't mean it. I think he is desperate to be with her.
I wonder what he would say if He knew what I was thinking.

Now here comes Deacon Jones with his long elaborate prayer, lasting 30 minutes. He looks so happy to be seen. I think he's a show off. After service, I'll tell him what an inspiring prayer he said.
I wonder what He would say if he knew what I was thinking.

Look back there, Sister Louise's daughter is home from college. I heard she's a straight A student, studying to become a doctor. Everyone thinks so highly of her. Well, they don't know what I know about her. That year she spent up in DC was not for studying. She had a baby and gave it up for adoption. I ought

to know, my son was its father, so she said. That ought to be my son in medical school. I don't understand why he didn't get accepted.
I wonder what He would say if he knew what I was thinking.

Brother Howard is about to make an announcement. He's doing so well with the new father-son group that he's leading. I told him last Sunday what a fine job he's doing, but he's only been a member here for six months. My goodness, I've been here for 16 years, I don't lead any groups. Of course, I really don't have the time.
I wonder what He would say if he knew what I was thinking.

The preacher's wife sure is smiling big this morning. Everything must be going her way. That dress she has on sure is flashy and gaudy. I'll ask her where she found such a lovely piece of clothing?
I wonder what He would say if He knew what I was thinking.

Here comes Trustee Tucker with one of his new ideas. I like things just the way they are! We don't need any change especially coming from him! He'll have to earn my respect. I'll tell the others, don't go along with a thing that he suggests. After service, I'll tell Trustee Tucker what great ideas he has.
I wonder what He would say if he knew what I was thinking.

Oops, the pastor has stepped on my toes. He said that people should be pure in heart, loving one another. I guess I'd better

pray. Lord, forgive me of my evil, jealous and
envious thoughts and forgive me of all my sins. I forgot, You
Know everything. You are omniscient!

Let the words that come out of my mouth and the thoughts of
my mind be reflective of the love that you put into my born again
heart, mind, and soul, because Lord, if you had come back for
your church today and reached for my hand and looked into my
heart, I wonder what You would have said.

MAKE ME WORTHY FOR YOUR KINGDOM

Lord, oh Lord, make me worthy
for Your kingdom.
Lord make me worthy for Your kingdom.
Lord, Oh, Lord, make me worthy that I may
sit with You in your kingdom one day.
Lord, open my eyes to Your Spirit so I can see Your heavenly
kingdom.

Lord, open my ears to your Spirit so I can hear
what's in Your heavenly kingdom.

Lord, open my heart to your Spirit so I can
feel and love You and Your heavenly kingdom.

Lord, please open my eyes, ears, and heart so that
I can understand the kingdom that You have
prepared — ready and waiting for those who believe.

Lord, please make me ready for Your kingdom!

OH JESUS, PLEASE TAKE MY HAND

Oh Jesus, Oh Jesus, please take my hand.
It seems like I'm walking in the middle of sinking sand.
I need you to help me to your solid land.

The sinful pleasures of life got me all in a bind.
Oh Jesus, Oh Jesus, please take my hand.
It seems like I'm having a lot of fun,
But I know it's not all right.
Please show me the light.

My soul belongs to You.
Oh Jesus, Oh Jesus, please take my hand.
I need to go to the Savior's School.
I don't want to be a fool.

Jesus, please give me a crown.
Now don't You show your frown
Oh Jesus, Oh Jesus, please take my hand.

Jesus, oh Jesus, I need You in my life.
Please don't let me out of Your sight.
Oh Jesus, oh Jesus, please take my hand.
Please take my hand, take my hand, take my hand.

REMEMBERING ME

Thank you for remembering me today
in such a special way.
Reflect for a moment on the love and good times
that we once shared here in God's house.
Keep the faith.
I stand in wait
when all of God's children will gather
in His kingdom.
Where there'll be
no more pains, tears, fears, night, or sea—
Just one big family with Jesus as our Light.

I WANNA GO

I wanna go to the place where there's no darkness.
I wanna go to the place where there's no sadness or tears.
I wanna go to the place where there's no fears or sins.
I wanna go to the place that is filled with love.
I wanna go to the place that is blessed with peace.
I wanna go to the place that is everlasting and beautiful.
I wanna go to the place with my God and see the throne
with Jesus Christ, my Lord,
Where there will be joy, joy, and more joy!

A MISSIONARY

Stand up, clap your hands.
Move your feet.
Say, Jesus, I'm a missionary!
Like you, I'm spreading the good news!

I am a missionary.
Like Jesus, I show love.

I am a missionary.
Like Jesus, I reach out and give to others.

I am a missionary.
Like Jesus, I help the sick and the lame.

I am a missionary.
Like Jesus, I pray on bended knees.

I am a missionary — I sing praises to my Lord, my God almighty.
Let your Holy Spirit keep on using me.
I'm steadfast in doing good works.
The Glory is all yours!

ONLY JESUS CAN FILL THIS HOLE

Pain, hurt, my night is hot tears.
The depth of my greatest fears.
The part of me that no one understands.
The spiritual shoulder to cry on.
Oh, Jesus, there's a hole in my heart,
that only You can fill, heal, close, or mend.

Let Your Spirit be my healer.
Please fill this hole in my heart.

The hurt feelings, wounds, of mind, body, and spirit—
Only You and I understand.

The misunderstandings, lack of confidence, doubt
pulling away into loneliness, guilt, grudges.
Lord, please fill this hole in my heart.
Seeing the dark, ignoring the light,
unable to recognize friend or foe.

Only You, Lord, can fill this hole.
Only You and I understand,
Only You, Lord, can fill this hole!

WHAT IS A MAN?

A man is kind, understanding, and patient;
A man is not afraid to show love for God and family.
He will stand tall and let his affections be known easily.

A man is not someone who has to sleep with one hundred women
to prove manhood, but is devoted and loyal to one woman.

A man loves his wife as Christ loves the church, and does not
mind pouring out his affinity to his wife humbly and without
false pride.

A man strives to provide for his family. He has neither to abound
in gold, nor be lazy and shiftless.

A man is not quick to criticize others. Instead, he thinks twice and
counsels privately to promote growth.

A man does not hold on to grudges, but is quick to forgive others,
just as Christ forgives us.

A man gives praise freely to others without envy and strife. He
does not wish frustration and failure upon anyone.

A man does not pray in elaborate fashion to impress others, but humbles himself and prays on bended knee from the heart and soul.

A man tries to keep peace in the house of the Lord, refraining from spreading gossip and emphasizing the failures and shortcomings of others.

A man is not always strong, bold, and courageous. Sometimes he cries too, and asks someone else for a helping hand.

A man does not look only to what benefits self, but to that which is in the best interests of those affected.

A man does not have to put on the most expensive raiment to feel good, but he derives more pleasure from the goodness of his heart and the deeds of his hands.

A man does not isolate himself, but instead, reaches out to others to help and finds a sense of fulfillment.

A man will not allow others to slander the character of a good person. He will speak up with the truth as he knows it.

A man sings from his heart and spiritual being, not to impress and win over others.

A man does the best he can.

He asks for forgiveness when he errs and does not get bogged down when criticized by others.

He knows what he has done, can do, and will do with God's help.

VICTORY IN JESUS

There is victory in faith, in my God, My Jesus
and the Holy Spirit.

If you believe that Jesus died on the cross
for you and arose from the dead,
then you can make the claim.
Your faith is the victory.

Victory, victory, victory!
Vic, vic, vic, victory, vic-to-ry!

If you have faith in my God, my Jesus,
and the Holy Spirit,
You can do all things.
You will never be left alone.
You will be blessed way down in your soul.
Your faith is the victory!

FIND MEANING IN YOUR LIFE

Go to Jesus to find meaning in your life.
You don't have to search anymore.
Jesus is all you need.

Go to Jesus to find meaning in your life.
Yes, go to Jesus to find meaning in your life.

Go to Jesus to find meaning in your life.
He'll protect you from all evil.
He'll fill you with divine joy.
Go to Jesus to find meaning in your life.

Go to Jesus to find meaning in your life.
Enjoy the victory of grace, faith, peace,
and salvation.

Go to Jesus to find meaning in your life!

GLORY DURING TRIBULATIONS

Give God the glory during your tribulations.
Give God the glory in hope, and faith, rejoice!

In his love, God will give you patience to endure.
Give God the glory during your tribulations.

God will show you his presence.

He'll make a way for you; look what He did
for Meshach, Shadrach, and Abednego.

Even the fiery furnace could do no harm.
Give God the glory during your tribulations.

DON'T YOU DOUBT

Don't you doubt, don't you doubt, don't you doubt
Don't you doubt.

My God said nothing is impossible
for those who believe-in Jesus Christ, my Savior.

It doesn't matter what the doctor or the lawyer said.
It doesn't matter what your family and friends said.

No matter what the situation,
Nothing is impossible for those who believe.

Don't you doubt, don't you doubt, don't you doubt,

Don't you doubt.

SECTION II

LOVE

A GIFT FOR THE WORLD

If I could give the world a gift, it would be the gift of love.
If there were enough love in the world, would there be so much violence, murder, rape, assault, theft?
If there were enough love in the world, would we have people wandering the streets without a place call to home?
Would the world have so much inflation
where medical assistance is unobtainable for many
because they are poor and so they die early an death?
While the world has a long way to go, something must be done to hurry the process and give us a lift.

Babies are born every day into a world where some may never know love. Some only exist with little or no food, clothing, or shelter. So you see why I would give the world a gift of love.

Think of this world where many schools have guns coming through their doors, but prayer is out. Criminals serve more time, in many cases, for stealing material things than for taking another's life.

Where are our values? Does the world indeed need a gift of love?

Are our world leaders honest and politically hard working or has corruption knocked at their windows and slipped through an opening?

How can people use drugs that kill their minds, and bodies, and erase hope and aspirations? Some grow it, manufacture it, and sell it to the poor who can't even afford to support their families.

Would a world filled with love allow this disaster to take place?

I would like to tell the world that God is love and He loves us. While many righteous may be afflicted, God can deliver all who believe in Him.

If I could give the world a gift, I would give it love overflowing like Niagara Falls —
beautiful rainbows colored all over the sky, and a sense of peace that is matchless.

INNOCENT LOVE

Innocent love
Oh innocent love
It feels so good.
It makes me happy.
Oh innocent love, love, love
I'm on top of everything.
Life is bigger than ever before.
My eyes sparkle and my heart sings of love.

You take my breath away.
Your kisses make my mind soar.
I feel safe tucked inside your arms.

You promised to keep me pure.
Innocent love
This is love for sure.
Innocent love, innocent love!

I THINK IT'S LOVE

It makes me feel full of energy.
It moves all through me.
This feeling makes me light and fluffy,
Like a cloud hanging around.
I think it's love, it might be love, I think it's love!

When I look into your eyes
I see the memories.
Cool walks, runs on the beach, quiet dinner.
A sad look in my mirror.
Coyness, novelty, sunrise, and sunset.
I think it's love, it might be love, I think it's love!

What can I do with this feeling?
On my knees, it weakens me.
Sweet kisses make me cry.
Even when times are difficult, I want to try.
Oh, don't let this feeling go away.
I've never felt this way.
I think it's love, it might be love, I think it's love!

CAN'T GET NO HOLD

Girl, you can't get no hold on my heart.
Your smile grips me, like a magnet.
But love can't swallow me now.
You know you've got to show how,
cause girl, you can't get no hold on me.

Your sweet smell of floral romance
leaves me somewhat rolled into a trance.
But girl, you can't get no hold on me.
No other girl I know can hold a candle to you.
Your wit, your beauty, your warmth—you're matchless.
But girl, you can't get a hold on me!

When we embrace, our hearts flutter,
and you feel so good.
I look into your gorgeous, sexy brown eyes
and slip into a dream.
But girl, you can't get a hold onto my heart!

You are so intriguing.
You keep me on my toes.
You're the best, not like the rest.
But girl, you can't get no hold on me.

IRONS IN THE FIRE

Baby, I gave you all that I had.
I put all my irons in the fire.
I told you all along, that all my love went to you.
I loved you almost more than God, more than the heavens,
but baby you dispersed it all to cloudy dust.

I put all my irons into the fire.
I gave you all that I had.
But you blew my feelings into the wind
and you never looked back.

On my knees, I fell, a grown man,
crying like I just came from my mother's womb.
all I saw was, you baby —
your fragrant smell, your soft touch
your sweet whisper in my ear.

Love, love, love baby I gave you all that I had.
If God heals my pain, I'll never love another like you.
Cause this is a one of a kind love for a fine and alive woman.
I put all my irons in the fire.
Oh baby, oh baby, how could you leave me?

You told me you'd always be here for me.
You had been so good to me.
After I met you, I felt confident inside.
I loved living, seeing the world with you.
Meeting important people, dining out
and, oh baby, the best was you.

I put all my irons in the fire.

I'm naked now.
Ashamed, want to hide somewhere.
Now, you are not here for me.
I gave you all that I had.
I put all my irons in the fire.

Ooh Baby, ooh baby.
I put all my irons in the fire.
I put all my irons in the fire.
Love, love, love, baby I gave,
Baby I gave, baby I gave you all that I had.

WHY DON'T YOU WANT ME BABY?

Why don't you want me baby?
You know you said you'd love me forever.
Now it seems like you want me never.
Why don't you want me baby?

You said you liked my sweet, sweet smell.
You even sang and brought me out of my shell.
Why don't you want me baby?

Last week, you held me real, real tight,
and you wouldn't let me out of your sight.
Why don't you want me baby?

You said I look pretty and fine.
Now you don't want to give me your time.
Why don't you want me baby?

You said I'm a different kind of gal.
You know the kind that makes you yell.
Why don't you want me baby?

You said I made you happy and all.
When you're with me, you feel mighty tall.

Why don't you want me baby?
You said I could lean on you to cry.
But you gave up on us and didn't even try.
Why don't you want me baby?

You know, you promised me an engagement ring.
Now you act like I'm just a thing.
Why don't you want me baby?

I really don't understand why,
I think you told me a lot of lies.
Why don't you want me baby?
You gave me that final good-bye call.
You acted kind of like you wanted to stall.
Why don't you want me baby?
Tonight, on bended knee, I prayed to my Father above.
Please help me get over this paradox called love.
Why don't you want me baby?
Why don't you want me baby?

HE'S GONE, MY MAN IS GONE

I didn't think it would happen.
Things changed so rapidly.
He's gone, he's gone, my man is gone.
I was only fooling myself.
Just didn't want to believe nothing was left.
He's gone, he's gone, my man, he's gone.
I felt it in his kiss.
I could see it in his eyes.
I could feel it in his touch.
The fire was gone.
I should've known
he would leave me all alone.
He's gone. He's gone.
My man, he's gone.
I can't hold these tears inside.
Our love was so much alive.
I just can't understand what happened to our love.
We thought it was a gift from above.
How could he fly away like a dove?
But, now he's gone.
He's gone.
My man is gone.

GIRL, IT'S A LOVE GAME

Girl, it's a love game
There's no man to tame
Don't give your love to no man
He'll give you a world of pain
Keep your feelings in the wind
Don't let that man get your mind
Cause Girl, it's a love game
The man is on the take
He'll put your heart on the stake
Forget those midnight kisses under the moon
You won't see that man no time soon cause
Girl, it's a love game, it's a love game
and it will never be the same
Girl, it's a love game
It's a love game
and it will never be the same
Girl, it's a love game
forget he ever even came
He won't make no promises to you
cause he's got more women to pursue
Those sweet words and caressing arms
are like honey bees ready to swarm
But girl you better not start to care
that man has many women to share

Cause girl, it's a love game
it's a love game
Girl, it's a love game
let him spend his money on you
It's better than his honey
it will soothe the pain when he is gone
Girl it's a love game
it's a love game

WHERE ARE THE GOOD MEN?

Where are the good men, my friend?
I can't find a good man to love.
No real love for me to capture.
Only my heart—left broken and all.
My friend told me that men are no good to the bone.
They have hearts of stone.
Just waiting to catch you alone
and string you along
so you can make your love song
filled with melodies of heartsick love.
They will treat you like a piece of wood
just to let you know you've been fooled.

Where are the good men, my friend?
I can't find a good man to love.
There are plenty of us good sisters
just waiting for that man to appear,
but his words never meant nothing but a wordy list.
Come on men, and get it together fast.
It's hard for sisters to last.
My friend said men never intend to be true
Because they are always looking for something new.

If it's not Gloria, or Brenda, he may be with you.
But you can bet, it'll never be just you.

Where are the good men my friend?
I'm still looking for that good man to love!

I JUST WANT TO LOVE AND BE LOVED

I feel sad, and empty, like a paper bag.
Wondering if anyone truly loves me.
I just don't understand why such hurtful things
have happened in my life.
I'm afraid to trust those who have shown me love;
I feel like I'm on the edge, swollen with anger
and ready for a fight!
Some people speak badly about me.
I'm not sure why.
I don't even understand why I'm here.
I've got some gifts, talents, but I don't know what to do.
Not sure what success is.
I don't use the same measuring stick as others.
Sometimes I have fun but not always in the best places.
I'm afraid to love and commit—
there's something called abandonment.
I really don't care what you think of me.
But deep down, I just want to love and be loved.
I just want to love and be loved.
Be loved, feel loved, know love.
I just want to love and be loved.

SECTION III

INSPIRATIONS

THE GREAT INTIMIDATOR

He is an uncomfortable ache in the belly —
A mountain of sweat.
He is the dread in the dark.
The shadow that lurks behind.
The bellowing crickets in the thickets.
He is the sword in the wakeful sleep.
The soft voice that confines and restrains
the spark that elicits the tremulous extremities
He is the biting flea in the sand.

Oh, where is your trust?
Where is your heart?
The stab of the great intimidator is upon you each
and every day.

The peace and pleasures of life are not complete.
Perhaps, it will all be swallowed up.

Take heed, enjoy today.
Stare fear in the face and spit him out as if he were poison
on the tongue,
and a viper who persists if you allow him.

BOLINDA

Bolinda was away from home for the first time.
She was off to a mostly white college and it's
1976 in the South.
Bolinda is smart but a timid black child.
She has the knowledge to do the work.
She prays daily to God and loves to go to church.
Bolinda's missteps were never overlooked.
She was placed on academic probation.
God told her to keep serving Him and she'd be alright.
Bolinda kept studying and staying up late in the night.
She remembered her humble home.
A mom who braided her hair and spanked her until she left.
Her family cast some doubts about her future goals.
Now she was on her own, but she knew God was on the throne.
Sometimes she felt like the people surrounding her
were of stone.
She knew God could soften their hearts and pour in his wonderful
Spirit.
Others praised her for her diligent endeavors and perseverance.
Classmates could finally truly see who she was.
They didn't have to look and see.
They felt her love and care.
Like picking up colored pencils,
they are different, yet all the same.

A GOOD WIFE

I am a good wife.
My grandmother told me that I would be.
She said I worked hard and was respectful to the elderly.
I saved 500 pennies. It was 1926.
I got married when I was sweet 16. I'm a woman now.
My husband was all that I dreamed of.
He was all that I prayed for — kind and Godly.
He was good looking and gave me some beautiful children.
I really loved my family.
God has blessed us.
We worked hard. We praised God.
We taught our children to lean on Jesus
And our Heavenly Father.
Every road will not be a good one,
But pray before you walk that way.
God knows about all of our days.
I guess we had the so-called American Dream.
Shall we say, a job, a home, a car, pretty good children,
and now some grandchildren and great grand's too.
I had nearly 60 years of marriage to the same man.
I am a good wife.
I have had to be strong when I knew things were going wrong.
I just kept on trusting in God and He has never let me down.
Early one morning, Jesus called me for my crown. I was ready.

HOORAY FOR THE BLACK MEN

Not all black brothers or men
are out there trifling and hanging out.
Many of our black men are well educated
have good jobs, and are great husbands and fathers too.

Isn't it a myth that most of our black men are in jail, jobless,
homeless, broke, divorced with children, or just burned out?

Hooray for our good Black men who step up to leadership,
strength, boldness, and know how to treat
our black sisters with love, gentleness and faithfulness.
Look into your history book.
See our black men who work at the White House, in the military,
In state government, and in city government.
Some are doctors, engineers, scientists, attorneys, business
owners, and executives.
The list goes on and on.
Our determined young black men can be anything they want to
become.

Let us keep supporting our young black boys and help them to
become strong,
well rounded black men.

Black men are mentors, fathers, role models, big
brothers and more.
Hooray for the black men.
Keep the black families thriving.
Hooray for the black men!

CIRCLES

I thought everything was in perspective:
romance, strong perfume, music, money,
status, excursions, hazy windows, burning lips,
and ice cream cones.

But what has happened now?
Murky clouds, cold winds, and sandstorms,
Fierce rains and snowy mountains

Can't touch anything,
can't hear the trumpet cry or the drum beats —
clear window panes, still can't see.

NEVER BE DEFEATED

In life, there will be some good times and some bad times too.
There will be some joy and some pain.
The key is to believe in God, and put Him first.
Our Lord Jesus will not let you down when friends, and even your parents or others might.
With God all things are possible.
There are no clouds so dense that God can't disperse the sunshine through.
Many times we suffer without need because we failed to
pray to Jesus.
You can do all things through Christ who gives you the strength.
No matter how bad things look, there is light at the end of the tunnel and
that Light is God.
There is always hope.
Believe in yourself.
God's got your plan and purpose.
Take one day at a time and live life to the fullest
But never at the expense of mistreating anyone.
Treat others the way you would want to be treated.
Never be defeated.
Whatever is going wrong, will pass.
Whatever you pray for, if it is God's will, it will happen.
Always have goals and direction in your life.

Ask of God, for his word is a compass, so study your Bible.
Surround yourself with people of good character,
Not with evil people who are quick to ignite
rage and problems.
Do not think of yourself as above or below others.
God created all of us.
Ask God to help you to discern what and who is best for you.
Don't worry about the future.
You know God is already there and has things all under control.
Trust that God will make all things work together for good
Because you love Him and He loves you.
Listen to God when he calls you to your purpose.
Accept that sometimes, things will not go your way,
but be assured and trust that God knows best.
He has a reason for it all.
You are not defeated.
God will see you through.
He's always on time.
He's your best shield in times of trouble.
God wants you to bring Him even the least of your concerns.
He wants you to involve him in every aspect of your life.
Believe and call his name, Jesus, Lord God!
Amen!

I LONG FOR A TASTE OF YESTERDAY

Sometimes I wish that I could sit once again beneath the huge weeping willow tree that fanned soft breezes against my young, tender cheeks.

I can hear my mother's hearty laughter as my sister joined the chuckle in an oh-so genuine way.

The smell of sugar cane still races past my nostrils. I can see the bright green leaves sway in the wind and kind of remind me of corn with long stalks.

I'd like to sink into the red clay and gently pat out mud pies with my brother nearby. Oh, what fun we had back then!

I can see the blackberries along a green, bushy path — muscadines and scuppernongs too, waiting to be made into pies by my mother's hard working yet gentle hands.

Sometimes I can feel my feet gliding gently over the softened gray dirt, treading rows ready to be planted with seed for fresh vegetables to be made into a chunky stew or sold at the downtown market.

I can hear the bees humming in their brownish gray nests and feel their painful sting on my little brown hand; here comes Mother, rubbing a pinch of tobacco all over it to heal my punctured wound.

The chickens and rooster that are going about their business, flapping wings, shedding grayish-black, white and yellow feathers always amused me. I knew to watch out for their scatterings on the ground. Yet it was all around.

The old big rooster, bold was he, climbed on to the squeaky porch and grabbed a red candy ball right out of my hand. Shattered was I, but so was he when Mother took an ax and showed me his gizzard.

Off to work went Dad in the early morning, but returned before darkness fell with treats like hot dogs, homemade ice cream, molasses, hoop cheese and brown ginger ale, just to name a few.

One TV did the entire family share, in closeness, we gathered in the front room with delight and complacency. Wrestling and boxing was a favorite for Dad.

Now it's church revival time, and good tasting food abounded like fried chicken, ham, potato salad, macaroni and cheese, green beans, chocolate cake, and ice tea.

The church services were fiery. The minister did preach fervently with fire and brimstone, raising a many shouts, cries, and songs. Lost souls took the front bench and many did pray as hand fans parted the hot air.

There are so many things and events that I long to visit again, drawing up buckets of fresh cold water, dancing in the rain, swimming in the lake, gathering tadpoles at the creek and catching bright bugs in a soda pop bottle.

In mind and spirit, the past I can revisit, but never again can I walk in yesterday; however, sometimes I still long for a taste of yesterday.

MY BLACK BABY DOLL

Momma said she's black like me.
Sometimes I put her in the mirror to see.
Her black hair is spongy like wool.
I bet that she wishes her hair like mine was cool.
She's got dark brown eyes, almost black.
Sometimes I wish my eyes were
light brown with sparkles instead of pecan brown.
But Momma said God made my eyes without a frown,
just the way he wanted them to be.
Just a thin line I see for my doll's eyebrows.
Mine are thick and heavy like the tail of a cow.
My doll's nose is not flat like mine.
I wish hers looked more like the African kind,
with pretty perched lips, just like my full ones.
My doll's a little like me, but she can't talk or cry.
I like to sing, clap, tap, hop and skip with my feet.
I wish my doll would try.
My doll can do none of these things, but
Momma said my doll is black like me.

VISITORS

They call me Mr. Crow
Cause I've got jet black skin and white teeth.
Here they come a knockin' on my door.
Don't know what they a coming here for.
They put on their best clothes.
Don't have to do nothing to impress me.
Gonna sit down on my sofa.
Probably gonna talk about the dust.
Don't like no visitors.
I know about a bunch of black folks
Sitting around telling a pack of lies.
Gonna look at you, hard
to see how your face changes.
They is looking for a payoff.
Ain't gonna get nothing here.

AN ANGEL IN GEORGIA

She was in her middle years and very ill.
She needed a new kidney because
her kidneys were both diseased and no longer working.
She said a prayer to God above and was certain
that a new kidney was on the way.
She got that new kidney one great day.
She was so grateful, kind, and reached out to others.
She told them the good news.
She was bright and enjoyed sharing
God's light with others.
The new kidney didn't work long.
Georgia said I have to stay strong.
God will make a way for me again.
Georgia prayed and got a second kidney.
She beamed and shared her story of
God's goodness and blessings.
Georgia's second kidney quit working too.
Georgia still praised God.
She shared His love and glory with all those who
came within her reach.
Her smile was contagious, and
her warmth was embracing.
Family and friends gathered around speaking of
all that Georgia had been through.

Georgia said God had her hand
and would lead her to his eternal land.
She breathed softly and took one deep breath.
A smile came upon her face.
Georgia had just left on her
Heavenly journey.
We, her family and friends observed her
peaceful smile.
We all realized that we had been blessed with
The presence of an angel in Georgia.

IT'S ABOUT THAT TIME

I came through the door with uncertainty on my mind.
I knew that I didn't have a lot of time.
Thank you for your smiles
that helped me live each day with the greatest stride.
You took the pain away that often started my day.
My suffering symptoms were alleviated as I opened
my eyes to see
It's about that time.
You took me, my family, and friends and opened windows
to help us plan things just the way we wanted them to be.
You've embraced our culture and we can see that
It's about that time.
I've enjoyed my humanitarian rights for comfort care.
My advanced illness has limited my life,
but not my soul.
I look back upon my life with great complacency, few regrets,
and nothing left unresolved.
I've made peace with those where conflict had dug a hole.
I know it's about that time.
Although, I can barely lift my head, feeling little attachment to my
environment,
I can feel the wind, smell the roses, see the sun through the murky
clouds and
recognize my God, there, across the river…I know it's that time.

A PICNIC TO REMEMBER

The best picnic of all time was the one my husband and I organized just before we moved to Augusta, Georgia, from Winston Salem, North Carolina. We were surrounded by family including parents, brothers, sisters, nieces, cousins, and close friends. The picnic was at a beautiful park.

There were various arrays of flowers, red, pink, white, and yellow. Red checkered tablecloths covered the long wooden tables. The grass was a beautiful deep green as the sun glistened over the lake. We had great food to eat such as ribs, corn on the cob, hotdogs, hamburgers, potato salad, baked beans ,watermelon and more. We even made homemade banana ice cream by hand turning on an old fashioned ice cream churn. The music and dancing was big fun. We rode paddleboats, went swimming and played old-fashioned horse shoe.

I remember my cousin, who was in his early twenties, running abruptly out of the cool lake water. He was yelling out in fear and then laughing heartily. He thought something in the water grabbed at his great toe. He almost lost his shorts as he

frantically ran onto land from the vast, yet serene lake. Yes, that was truly a great picnic back in June of 1980. The fond memories will live forever within my heart with warm impressions of everyone who attended. Just as the last few of us were leaving, my husband peered up at the loft of the shelter and there lay a rattlesnake. Thank God, he slept through the whole thing.

MY PHILOSOPHY OF LIFE

My philosophy of life begins with understanding myself. I believe that I was created in my mother's womb by God. I believe that he has a plan for our lives. One of the most important areas of life is to recognize that God is our higher power. If we seek God first, all of the other things in life will fall in place. We need to have a personal relationship with God to understand life. We need to follow our own star, for it is not meant that we all receive the same blessings and gifts. We must trust God to direct our footsteps and believe that we can do all things through Him, who can provide us with all the resources that we need. We must love our neighbor. We need to stay interested in others and be helpful. If one does not know his mission in life, it is to spread God's word, to help the poor, to visit the sick and the imprisoned. I also believe in embracing life and enjoying life. I enjoy doing new things such as traveling to see as much of this beautiful world as possible that the Lord has created. I believe in the end, love will be the most important thing to have experienced. It does not matter whether it is altruistic love, family/friend love, or romantic love; we just need to love one another. We need to be humble because we are all equally great in God's family. We need to recognize that some people will only be in our lives for a season and we should recognize God's purpose in that. We should recognize that there will be some challenges, some trials, pain and sorrow in life, but

with a higher power, He will see us through. We need to take time to appreciate the little things in life, and the special people that God has placed in our lives. We must trust God to turn ill will into victories. We should strive to live our lives in a way that we can look back without regrets. We need to pray for the motivation to change the things that we can and recognize that God is our protector and comforter. We need to forgive and be forgiven. By all means, we should never give up on hope. There is always light at the end of the tunnel and that Light is God, my and your Lord Jesus.

ABOUT THE AUTHOR

Carolyn Walker was born in Greensboro, NC. She has been writing since age eleven. She recognized her talent for writing when she won an essay contest on soil erosion in the sixth grade. In the ninth grade, she won the Daughters of American Revolution play writing contest. In the eleventh grade, she won a short story contest at her high school, Southeast Guilford. In college, she published poems in the college booklets or newsletters in both undergraduate and graduate school.

She graduated from High Point Memorial Hospital School of Nursing with a diploma in 1976 and is the only minority graduate of that school. She obtained her BSN degree in nursing from Winston Salem State University in 1980 and her Master of Education from Augusta College in 1984.

Through the years, Carolyn continued to write poems, songs, short stories and started writing a novel, which she has published, God Hears, Sees, and Blesses. Carolyn is now working on her third book, a novel and is working on a collection of short stories for children and young adults.

She married J. Odell in 1979 and their daughter was born in 1983. She retired after thirty-seven years of nursing and plans to devote her retirement years to writing, singing, and speaking about God's goodness in the lives of herself and others.

www.ingramcontent.com/pod-product-compliance
Lightning Source LLC
Chambersburg PA
CBHW031606040426
42452CB00006B/422